Positive Discipline Techniques

Positive Discipline Techniques

Table Of Contents

Foreword

Chapter 1:
Discipline Basics

Chapter 2:
Consider Where Your Child Struggles

Chapter 3:
Use Age Appropriate Consequences

Chapter 4:
Be Clear About Expectations And Consequences

Chapter 5:
One Firm Warning Is Enough

Chapter 6:
Don't Give In And Be Consistent

Chapter 7:
The Consequences Of Incorrect Discipline

Wrapping Up

Foreword

Everyone needs to have some form of discipline embedded into their lives to create a smoothness that will help the person function in an acceptable manner. Most of these discipline elements are adopted from a very young age and usually initiated by the parents of the child. In order to teach the child how to eventually simulate into society and be manageable, these discipline measures are necessary. Get all the info you need here.

Positive Discipline Methods

Chapter 1:
Discipline Basics

Synopsis

The following are some of the basic discipline philosophies that are usually introduced to a child from a very young age:

The Basics

Good discipline is not about working out punishments, as this does not really teach the child about the actual negativity of the act that required some discipline attention.

Instead it really teaches the child that the stronger component in the equation usually get to dictate and cause the weaker one to simply follow along.

Good discipline measures are meant to teach a child right from wrong and not simple address the wrong. Making the child understand self control and socially acceptable behavior is one way of encouraging the method of good discipline.

The parent will show agreement of good behavior with praising and encouragement and will usually address bad behavior with the opportunity to discipline using respect, patience and good problem solving skill as opposed to simply working out punishment.

Good discipline is not about going through the process of a power struggle. When a child is much younger it may seem acceptable to use this kind of discipline but as the child grows older it would definitely be much more difficult to use this style as the older child will more likely retaliate, thus making the already difficult situation worse.

Good discipline does not mean making the child feel insulted or suing demeaning elements to cause hurt. Using styles such as yelling and name calling will not help the child in any positive way.

Chapter 2:

Consider Where Your Child Struggles

Synopsis

Every child has problems in certain areas in their lives which may cause some disciplinary requirement in order for these problems not to escalate out of control. However it is not always easy to understand the child's position and problem and working out some form of discipline without a thorough understanding will only make matters worse.

Where Help Is Needed

Often children will emulate what they have observe from those closest to them, thus most of the struggles a child experiences will eventually be solved the way they see the parents or adults around the do so.

Therefore in the quest to try and help the child through the problems and the methods used for suitable solutions, every consideration should be given to understating why the child has a problem in a particular area to being with.

The following are some of the ways that can be adopted when working out discipline while still being very aware of the areas the child struggles in:

Decide how to handle the situation without further adding to the problem. Take step that would reinforce discipline but at the same time the method used should also allow the child to understand and accept, things are being done, taking their best interest to heart.

Using firmness but salting it with kindness will go a long way in assuring the child that the parent understands the struggle, but does not condone the behavior being shown on the part of the child. Nurturing through disciple may seem like a strange concept to follow but will be effective in the long run as it does not aim to bring done the child natural spirit and zest for life.

Having family meeting to address the problem will also help to show the child that his or her feelings and struggles are being considered and are important to all. This will help the child accept the discipline measures with less chances of rebellion.

Chapter 3:
Use Age Appropriate Consequences

Synopsis

In order to discipline a child properly, there should ideally be some thought given to how the parent should go about the action and what type of action should be considered. Simply working out punishment for the sake of disciplining a child will not be productive at all and may sometimes even have a destructive result.

The Right Discipline

The following are some guidelines that can help to make the choice of discipline measure more appropriate to both the child's age and to address the act that required the discipline is a suitably corresponding and appropriate manner:

The parent should consider the development stage the child is going through. This should be on an individual basis as this may differ greatly even in the same age group.

Reading books and other material on this may be helpful in steering the parent in the right direction.

Start building a good foundation for behavioral patterns. Ensure the child understands from a very early age what is acceptable and what not acceptable behavior is.

Dealing with this before there is actually a need to address any inappropriate behavior by working out disciplinary action will be better for the child as the child will not be confused by the sudden onslaught of the negative reaction from the parent.

Understanding the brain development in general is also important as it important that child be able to comprehend the disciplinary action taken and not perceive it as usually cruel and uncalled for.

The parent should be able to understand that at certain ages the child will react to things in a certain manner that is out of their own comprehension, thus the need to understand the brain development processes before actually working out punishment. Obeying something that they can really comprehend will be difficult for the child.

Chapter 4:

Be Clear About Expectations And Consequences

Synopsis

The first thing a parent should understand is that children are not born instantly knowing all rules and regulations in life. This they will learn mostly through trial and error and it is the duty of the parent to teach these, in the best way possible preferably without causing any damage to the child mentally or physically.

Be Clear

The following are some guidelines that can help the parent understand how to ensure the child is clear about the expectations and consequences before there is a need for discipline:

Both parties should be able to understand and accept that the discipline worked out is not meant to solely represent punishment but is to help the child curb the need to act in a particular way in the future.

This will help the child understand that the punishment or discipline measure taken is not meant to hurt or harm neither is it all about the power.

The idea behind the action taken should clearly show the child the expectations and consequences that are directly related to a particular act only and nothing else.

Confusing the child with non connective elements will not help the child separate the various acts and the discipline measure taken especially if the child is very young and as for the older child, there is the likelihood of resentment building when unfairness is perceived.

The child should be made to understand that the expectations of the parents and adults around, is not about a power struggle but about molding the child for future simulation into society and making the transition easy and enjoyable.

Being consistent in the disciplinary actions worked out and also taking these measures as soon as possible after the offending behavior is displayed in very important. The younger the child if swifter the action taken to ensure the child understands the connection between the action and the punishment.

Chapter 5:
One Firm Warning Is Enough

Synopsis

Sometimes there is a need to simply step back from the actual need to give out any sort of punishment or disciplinary action and just give the child a firm warning. However parents, who choose to use this method, should learn that there should also be consequences to be accepted and expected should the initial firm warning not be adhered to or taken seriously.

Only Once

There are several ways the firm warning technique can play out and this may include some of the following thought processes:

Natural consequences – in this particular scenario the parent's job is to firm warn the child of certain measures that should be taken for the convenience of the child and if these measure are not taken, the parent will not step in and compensate for any loss or negative occurrences.

The child will be taught that the firm warning is all the help he or she is going to get and will have to work with the results of their actions.

Logical consequences – this is another way the parent can tackle a situation with just a firm warning. Taking the time to explain to the child the consequences of different actions before the child is put in a position where he or she would have to react is one way of being firm, as the parent's explanation should ideally also include the extent of help to be expected from the parent and nothing more.

This will also help the child make decisions on just how much they are prepared to handle and if such actions are worth the possible negative consequences which they will have to deal with themselves and accept.

Positive discipline – here the parent will not only explain the consequences but will assure the child that the consequences will be worked out without any hope of compromise.

Chapter 6:

Don't Give In And Be Consistent

Synopsis

Disciple is really is rather hard for a parent to consistently participate in especially when the parent is either usually never around or when the child is clever enough to seem innocent when the time for disciplining comes around.

Keep Going

However parents should understand that all discipline should have some form on consistency, in order to be effective on any level. There is also the important of making the child understand this attitude of consistency so that he or she will understand that every action has a consequent reaction be it positive or negative.

If the parents are able to be consistent and stand their ground no matter what, the children will soon learn the importance of weighting their actions before actually acting upon them. This will eventually makes things easier for both parent and child.

Being consistent and steadfast in the discipline area will also help the younger child understand the particular behavior or action is not going to be tolerated and thus will slowly wean themselves off.

However if the discipline is not consistent the child will learn to maneuver the situation according to the parent's mood swings thus teaching them how to cunningly get their way.

Besides this the child will also be very confused when the disciplinary action is not consistent and the child will not really be able to understand the enormity of the negative act if the punishment worked out differs considerable each time.

Trying different types of punishment in order to make the child understand the negative act is unacceptable is alright but the disciplinary action worked out should be along similar lines of severity so that consistency can be effectively maintained at all times.

For the parent, keeping to this consistency will also make their job much easier and predictable and this is an important feature to incorporate in the child's mind.

Chapter 7:

The Consequences Of Incorrect Discipline

Synopsis

There are several dangers connected to the incorrect discipline methods a parent may decide to use and below are some of the possible repercussions of such erroneous decisions:

Important Points

If the child is too young to understand to mode of discipline being given out, the confusion will not allow the child to actually focus on the negative act that caused the need for discipline but will cause the child to focus on the fact that maybe the parent does not really love or care for them after all.

This is very damaging for a young child and can be far reaching effects that maybe so embedded in their subconscious that it may be difficult to change.

Incorrect discipline may also cause the child to feel inferior and therefore eventually become very withdrawn. This may also erode their self- esteem.

A child with low self esteem issues will also end up having problems in other parts of their life, thus creating even more problems in the long run.

If the disciple usually takes on a physical mode, then the child will eventually learn or perceive the only way to get what they want is to be physical about it.

Therefore they will constantly resort to physical displays of violence as they perceive this to be the accepted way to get things done their way. All this is due to the example first set by the parent in the style of discipline used.

Incorrect form of discipline can also make a child feel resentful towards the parent thus causing friction within the family unit. Sometimes this can result in relationships going bad.

Wrapping Up

The time should fit the crime is a popularly touted saying that most people would understand. Therefore when it comes to disciplining children this same concept should also be adhered to.

www.ingramcontent.com/pod-product-compliance
Lightning Source LLC
LaVergne TN
LVHW020508080526
838202LV00057B/6238